POETRY IS MINDFULNESS

POETRY IS MINDFULNESS

BY DAVID CHURCHILL

POETRY IS MINDFULNESS

© 2016 David Churchill

Cover art: "Modern Family" by Kevin Sloan
Book layout by Barbara Shaw

Second Edition

Published by:
Pony One Dog Press
PO Box 30552
Bethesda, Maryland 20824

for Theodoric

Strange how people who suffer together
have stronger connections
than people who are most content—

Bob Dylan, *Brownsville Girl*

Contents

Poetry is Mindfulness, the Essay

Perhaps a better title for this essay might have been "Poetry is Mindfulness, *the Defense*," for at first glance it might appear as if I too am trying to cash in on the mindfulness movement. Indeed a backlash against its exploitation appears to have arrived. The marketing of special teas (Mindful Lotus tea, $6 for 20 bags) to apps you can download to your iphone (Headspace, $13 a month for guided mindfulness exercises), prompted David Gelles to remark recently in the New York Times, "If mindfulness can be bought as easily as a pair of Lululemon yoga pants, can it truly be a transformative practice that eases the troubled mind?" The answer of course is still "yes." Just because something is exploited doesn't mean it isn't worth exploiting; rather, as in this case, the reverse: what was originally one aspect of a lifelong journey is still very much a skill to be acquired.

What this book urges instead is a consideration of poetry. Poetry has always been mindful. Just as mindfulness has always existed—before Donovan, before crystals or New Age, before the Beatles went to India—"secular" mindfulness has also always existed. It simply had a different name. It was called "verse."

As a form of virtual reality that "exists in a space", as I have proposed in a different place, poetry's aim has always been to situate its readers in the present moment, even if that moment is only a "moment" in the poem. More, it has aimed to coax the moment to open, as a flower opens. Whether through the medium of print or the spoken word, poetry has always promoted the observation of thoughts, emotions and sensations. Like an incantation, poetry is itself a form of meditation that can lead to peace of mind, greater self-awareness, reduced stress, improved focus, many and perhaps even more of the same benefits claimed for mindfulness.

The kind of poem referred to here as "mindful" however, is a special kind of poem. The purpose of this essay is to discuss that poem, as I conceive of it. I will attempt to describe the type of poem that is particularly mindful, that is, one whose effect is exactly to produce mindfulness. And I shall do this under two heads. For convenience sake, assume one aspect of a poem is "spiritual", the other "physical."

The "spiritual" aspect of the mindfulness poem refers to the creator of the poem, the poet. Specifically, it refers to the inwardness of the poet, his or her creative process, his or her state of mind, and what takes place in that state during the inception, genesis and writing of the poem.

The creative mindset is always going to be somewhat mindful anyway, at least from the perspective of other callings. The creative person will be the one watching a flock of birds in the sky, following a formation of clouds overhead or just watching a nest of ants boiling up from a crack in the sidewalk, long after others with perhaps less time on their hands have moved on. This is the kind of mindfulness that holds the distractions of the work-a-day world at bay for a moment or two, while maintaining a state of being focused on precisely the act of being unfocused. But the kind of creative mindfulness from which a mindfulness poem arises, including all of the above as it does, yet includes something else in addition. The mindfulness poem arises out of a particular kind of creative mindfulness.

The poet Robert Bly, in a book titled *Leaping Poetry: An Idea with Poems and Translations,* calls the sort of poetry that emerges from the kind of mindfulness I have in mind, "leaping poetry". I have never cared very much for this term, but inasmuch as it is something that will supply an indication of the kind of mind that can produce it, we should retain it for the present and look at what Robert Bly means by it.

He says, "My idea, then, is that a great work of art often has at its center a long floating leap, around which the work of art in ancient times used to gather itself like steel shavings around the magnet. But a work of art does not necessarily have at its center a single long floating leap. The work can have many leaps, perhaps shorter. The real joy of poetry is to experience this leaping inside a poem. *A poet who is 'leaping' makes a jump from an object soaked in unconscious substance to an object or idea soaked in conscious psychic substance.*

"Thought of in terms of language, then, leaping is the ability to associate fast. In a great ancient or modern poem, the considerable distance between the associations, the distance the spark has to leap, gives the lines their bottomless feeling, their space, and the speed of the association increases the excitement of the poetry."

He goes on to claim that by the end of the nineteenth century, energy in poetry began to come more and more from the unconscious, and that both poem and dream had been set free. Poets had begun to devote their lives to deepening the range of associations in the poem, and increasing the speed of association.

This then is what characterizes the special type of process that gives rise to the mindfulness poem. A poet who is doing this is writing out of "the human shadow". The concept of the shadow goes back to Jung. It is the part of ourselves that is hidden from us. It is the "long black bag we drag behind us", filled with all the things we have been taught from childhood to dislike or fear about ourselves. Jung also maintained it was the place in each of us where our own hidden personal energies, perhaps feminine for men, masculine for women, were mingled with the dark, hidden, forbidden, perhaps even Satanic energies of our race. The poet who thus joins within himself the energies of the dark, shadow-cloaked side of himself with the well-lit subjects of the waking world, such as mathematics and geometry, is most likely to be writing mindfulness poems.

So much for the "spiritual" aspect of the mindfulness poem. What then is its "physical" aspect? What does it look like on the page? What kind of work does it do, what kind of effect does it make? How will I know one when I read it?

First of all, the mindfulness poem is usually not a very long poem. How long? Just long enough to do its job. And what is its job? Its job is to bring its reader to a state of mindfulness. —*Then let the reader go.*

The mindfulness poem is a poem that releases the reader after the reader has read it. That is its primary qualification. It may also be descriptive and/or narrative in style. Its primary action is to shift the reader from the virtual reality of the poem to the external reality of the reader's surroundings. It is like the puff-breath that sets the fluff of the dandelion whirling in the air. It sets the reader going with refreshed senses and a sharpened sense of perception. It brings the reader to a heightened sense of awareness. But it cannot contribute to mindfulness unless it is also able to release the reader once he or she has achieved that state. It cannot do this unless it is able to let the reader go.

The mindfulness poem aims to produce a state of heightened awareness. It then, like Dante on the mountain of Purgatory, will be found to have vanished, even while you held its hand.

In conclusion, I am not a purist. If I am correct in my belief that the purpose of poetry is to improve experience, then its method must surely be by transaction. I believe a poem should be—and rightly is—*other*-focused. Thus the poem as I conceive it is a transaction. The fact that you and I may not know each other doesn't change this. The poem acquaints us. The standing of the poem on its own merits, as in a formal, New Criticism sort of way, is secondary. Past time the pendulum swung back.

A poem is a gift. It is a gift from a poet to a reader. It is about something the poet can give you to help you pass the time. It is about something to do while waiting for a bus, something to entertain you, something to do between "checking Instagram and starting the next episode of House of Cards", to quote from

David Gelles again. The mindfulness poem in particular is a gift, a giving of awareness. Its function is clearly to transfer creative mindfulness from one person to another. It is, in a sense, a one-way transaction—but only in a narrow sense. In a broader sense, it truly is a two-way experience.

POETRY IS MINDFULNESS

Meridian Hill Park

Statue of Jeanne D'Arc, April, 2016

Here, above the city,
where from this cliff
a battle-clad girl
leads her army of air
into the sky,

a medieval faire has appeared,
as if brought to life
by her charge,
though Moroccan drums
know nothing
of divine passion,
unless spring is divine:

here is the joy of playing
cards on the grass,
and obedient dogs
conjoined to their owners,
and children
tasting freedom—

all brought to life
by a sustaining sun.
No one sees
the young woman behind them,
steel-clad toes

rising lightly
in the stirrups,

highlighted by azure—
We do not even
know her beautiful
back,
that has a different
death in mind,
turned on our bliss,
entirely of this earth.

Zoo Walk

It was the kind of day I adore:
clouds floating in
languid pools
overhead in the blue,
trees gilded
by a single brush,

and enough left over
to fill the air with
tenuous gold—
so I did the only thing
a sane person
could do,
I went to the zoo.

If you want to see something,
look inside cages:
a few carrots on the floor,
an overturned water-tin;
that is the place
for looking at wildlife . . .

Not where bamboo fades
in a weave of silk,
whisper of cataracts
and crags
more present in mind
than geography . . .

Pandas are disguised
as shadows
on snowbanks,
the dolphins are waves.

One species doesn't care
if animals are happy
in their habitats;
no chance of missing
them at the zoo:
the sunlight
is pregnant with them,
birthing them

in their leisure hordes,
shadowy forms
condensing out of gold—
Existence itself
is a habitat,
and *they* appear at home . . .

Homeless God Bless

He no longer stands
on corners and curbs.
He no longer looks in windows.
He no longer holds
out his hand like
a handshake to life.
He no longer expects
anything of us.
He lies on the step
of a boarded-up door.

You in the doorway,
what do you think about?
You never speak.
Are you shut in?
I don't believe
you can even talk
to yourself anymore:
silence is so thick in you,
if a pin dropped
it would stop
before hitting the floor.

For some men the
descent for Eurydice
only gets as far as this:
a bottle of cheap
wine and a packet

of bath-salts
that never lets them go.
But I believe loneliness
can do this too.

The window is open
and the outdoors breathes
in on spring air
clear as a glass of Chablis.
Reflections live in
the wine on the table,
and voices ring
in the singing of forks,
speaking of cleaning
products and the
latest new restaurants . . .

Dog-tags jangle outside
and water splashes:
a water-bowl pulls
the mild street into
its skin, but lets the dog go—
He has no need
of a leash. His soul links
him to everything,
and everything to him:
sleepy puppy-eyes
seem to ask,

how is it possible
loneliness even exists?

From where the man
in the doorway lies,
the question is answered:
the crowds hurrying
to work, each one
a uniquely fitted key,
each to his own keyhole—
All searching in vain
for the one key
that opens every door—

But when day fades
and night brings on
its partitions of dusk,
I skirt bars and
tattoo parlors, pass
unseen by crowds
on carpets of light—
Friendly people know
the truth:
there are no keys,
no keyholes,
and doors are closed . . .

Genesis 2:4
for Pamela Stardust

Was Eden a real place?
Take me to the rolling
hills of the high veldt
country, where I can stare out
over tawny hill-flanks
that breath in the heat,
and let me stand in the shade
of umbrella-acacias,
and ask me again—

Some say a place
where four rivers flowed
is under cerulean today,
where tracks of the rivers
can be traced in the desert
that abounded with game,
when the desert was green
and sea-levels low,
though others say elsewhere . . .

The Tower of Babel was real,
Herodotus saw it—
Mount Ararat is real,
as were any number of floods,
though Christians have carried
splinters of the Ark
to their homes long ago,

souvenirs of the sacred,
still to be seen
in any number of churches—

And every child knows
exactly where Eden was.
No guardians were needed
to keep us away,
no expulsion required:
that first pang
of childhood shame
like a flash of cold
light changes everything,
and never dims—

Yes, Eden *was* real—
Though we can
no longer return,
we can still walk around,
see what it looked like . . .

Walking Mindfulness

I have taken my temperature.
I am running a fever.
I am not feeling myself.
I believe I am ill.
I am ill out of everyday life.

Sudden noises disturb me.
Cars are in auras.
I am out of my skin.
Trees are full of birds
and leaves are
chattering about it.

A street-man shuffles by
in broken-down shoe backs
and judo pants:
where is *his* mind?
Not in this world—
A private wind blows
his thoughts to
jumbled calendars,
above the house-tops.

People are bumping me,
I'm in everyone's way—
But pigeons are joy-flocking
over the intersection,
and that's done it—

I'll be here for an hour.

I don't want to move anyway.
I just want to stand here.
I am a single eye.
How long can I survive?
I'll slip into a coffee-house
till this illness subsides.

What I Learned in the Suburbs
Germantown 1986 - 2011

The blind do not walk in the dark—
Blindness could be a room
where every wall
is painted white.
Likewise for the sighted,
levels of non-sight.
You could look at
the habitat in yourself
and see nothing but trees,
feelings in disguise.

In certain suburbs, that's all there is:
cicada wings,
downed tree limbs,
people waiting for buses . . .
To live in this place
you must agree to be inward.

A license plate said,
 "Know Thyself"—
So I made a religion
of knowing myself:
I was knowing myself
at the child-care house,
where the child-care woman
who was called by the Lord

took my picture every day
before she allowed me
to leave with my child,

and I was knowing myself
when the mainstream-boy
knocked out her teeth
because he didn't know what love
was—

So I went down
to the bottom of the hill
with an idea in mind,
to find out where I lived:
not by the map, but by the land,
before hills became problems
for engineers to solve—

Men were mowing their pastures
and buffing their wagons,
and life seemed to have fallen
asleep in the heat—
Doing anything different
was entirely impossible . . .

So I went down through the houses,
past the family that sets
a place at their table

for Jesus, and the neighbor
who bends spoons,
to the bottom of the hill,
and went into a shade
of colonial basswoods . . .

The forest exhaled
and I stood in a cavern
of sunlight dissolved,
and birds were like twigs
in spring-water,
and the sky was a sink-hole
in the trees
and everything floated . . .

A bird was before me
as if in a spotlight,
the tails of its coat above its legs,
balancing its beak
on a loop of its neck.

The closest I ever came
to another person
was the face of a woman
in a reflection of my own
in the window of a store.
Had she looked up,

I could have breathed in her eyes.
I moved on when she turned—

But in that stream for a moment
two animals stared
at each other:
not love, exactly—
but a kind of contentment
two souls can feel
when they don't have to talk . . .

Then show-feathers fanned
as if it remembered
it had elsewhere to be,
and languidly it lifted,
shaking its wings
as if to shake off their weight . . .

Then he was gone . . .
And I was glad to see him fly.

Nocturne

All Hallows' E'en
Germantown, 2009

It was calm all day,
but a wind came up,
rattling the tree-tops:
oak leaves,
leaves of the sycamore,
maple,
leaves blowing and falling.

When night fell
the wind finished its work:
bat-loops in lamp-light.

Then they came knocking:
down the block
they came knocking,
across the street
they came knocking,
To the back
they came knocking,

children came knocking,
hungry children, knocking . . .

My Life as a Patient

This is what I'm told:
the last thing we do,
before leaving the world,
we drink from a river.

Where the river is,
what it's called,
how they get there—
this I don't know.
But I know you can see it.

Watch the old man
alone in the chair.
He no longer remembers
the names of his sons;
his wife is a stranger—
He started early
taking sips from the river . . .

Is it bitter, the taste?
Is it something
to get used to?
Or are you afraid
of forgetting too much,
too fast—?

They stay just long enough
to drink,
then close their eyes
and depart—
while we too disappear,
fading before them . . .

Better to begin now
to forget them—
Nothing holds us
anyway,
but intimate thorns,
easiest to tear away from . . .

I too must have drunk
from that river:
I look in old journals,
see words
I no longer understand,
in a hand
I can no longer read.

Who was that failed writer
at eighteen—
That young men
disappointed in the world
at twenty—
That thirty-year-old,
eating himself alive—?

Where has the husk
of the locust gone,
clinging to a tree-branch—
where is the skin
of the snake,
skeined among the stones
of a tumbling wall—?

The locust has flown,
 the snake has wound away . . .
And an old man is on a hill,
counting the feathers
in the flying wing. .

Rainstorm
June 22, 2016
23red & L Sts NW

The rain is in sheets
on the windshield,
and if the wipers were propellers
you would be air-borne:

all you can see
are the leaves overhead,
nodding in agreement
to the drumbeat,

and a girl at the curb,
standing in floodwater
with a bouquet of roses.

I know life and death
are opposites,
must exist together:
living, we know death,

so too in death
there must be life;
Nature knows it too—
it will tear the sky
down
to water those roses.

Corcoran Street
Washington DC Spring, 2016

Everything is lifting you up
on this street:
pink and white petal
balloons that are leaking
their helium
are making you float,
but at least *they*
are still tethered to the ground.

Instead you are up
among house-tops
where Victorian adventures begin,
with close-ups
of balconets,
birds under eaves,
bird-troughs
like vines that point the way down.

Underneath,
people are hurrying to work
or running late,
heads down:
everything important
is under their feet—
Our future is overhead,
where sparrows call
continually for mates.

Who would not
want to live on this street?
Someone has left
a box of books
out to keep.
Forget corbelled turrets
floating
into cumuli—
When these trees
are in leaf,
this street will be rich.

Museum Guard

This room is backward:
its many windows
admit no light.

Ten views of canals
and spires pricking clouds,
barefoot girls
at the edge of a marsh,
and cows.

The light of the room goes
to illuminate those.

What's it like working here,
I ask the guard.
Her eyes search
for a blank scrap of canvas.

Nod if art
has any interest for you . . .

—Or is it better not to speak
any languageat all?

World in Need

Gray wind going around
like a carousel
of shacks and billboards—

A gray tilt-a-wheel
full of believers
strapped in their pews,
reels past burning houses,
lands under water—

What is happening in America?
A fire is burning
from Oklahoma to Kansas:
abandoned theme parks
are smoldering
like paint in a coal-stove.

The desert is coming
like an unwelcome neighbor,
the turf is dying
and the grass is dirt.

Snow and high winds blow
across the plains:
every door in America
opens on a drift.

We do not yet know
something is born—
The children of history
are born
in the silence of gunfire,
the whispers of blasts.
We spend our time
in a waltz
with the whirlwind,

waiting for help
from manifesting angels.

A carnival has come
to a field by the tracks,
filling the night
with laughter and shrieks . . .

You can hear the groaning
of the engines
that keep the rides churning,
behind the backs
of the crowd,
when you stand there alone . . .

Beach Walk, After Storm

The wind boomed,
throwing the gulls about,
and blew a life-form
out of the waves:
a fortress of claws.
It struggled to right itself,
exposed on the sea-bed—

crawled to a piece of glass
the sea had coughed up,
turned and backed in,
tried to close its door with a claw,
glad to find boundaries
in an unbounded place.

A wave came again to my feet.
I watched it search
for the crab in the cruet,
find and reject it—

But the next wave forgave it
and another embraced it
and gathered it in
and the sea seemed to cradle it,
full of pity for things
that take shelter
where they can find it—

I went on then,
in a world made of glass,
seeing through the rain
and the wind
and the waves when they thin,
and counted myself lucky . . .

Till we grow old—
and one of those dreams
of ours,
in the middle of the night,
turns into a new life . . .

Coming of Age

for Amanda,
Coming of Age COA-MAT celebration.

Sometimes it is a door
you go through.
Sometimes it is two trees
by a road.
Sometimes it is
the open arms of a friend.

Mostly there is no turning
sword or cherubim
to tell you
you are grown;
but an infant's footprint
in a sidewalk,
when the walk was poured,
sometimes hints.

Or sometimes this:
a place where leaves
like serpent scales
hide wasting fruit,
and cold birds screech
in stone,
and shadows creep
across a span of dates,

and you, alone,
feeling the downdraft
on a frozen wing . . .

Pornography Circus

"Is the tired of looking at shtampovanyye,
samey body with the chipper breast is the
standard hot the body, which used to
the sexual attraction . . . "
   Look at Me, translated from Russian

Everybody likes
some low-rent love-boy
or dumb blond;
it makes no sense to me—
No one wants
to get it on with a genius . . .

I think it goes back
many thousands of years,
when Neanderthals
were interbreeding among us:
we are descended
from a people
who didn't like them too bright.

Red-heads got their hair
and the rest of us
their immune system—
Two years later
my red-headed lover
who never gets a cold
turns into my sister.

Intimacy is always incestuous—
But in the beginning,
before even love
was invented,
there must have been two people,
alone in nature,
whose only desire
was to fulfill a commandment.

Dumbarton Oaks
Summer 2015

So much depends on
the time of the year
when you come to the garden.

In winter it is cold
but in summer
you can close your eyes

and let your nose be your guide:
it will lead you
through fireless embers,

Easter eggs on stalks
and fragrant cow-licks,
through iris frills

and candy-colored crusts;
past every forgotten
memory of childhood . . .

past a gardener-couple
at work in the beds,
and a presence of breeze,

as though someone
were walking beside you,
and always the trebles

of fountains,
basins and pools
you could drink with your eyes,

make you believe
you could live here forever . . .
—Until you go down,

down the Box Walk,
past the Ellipse,
past the Seat of Two Friends,

where the garden ends
at the bottom of the hill,
where the hills

of forsythia end:
an arch-gate,
remembered only

by envious ivy,
walled up with cinder-blocks,
speaks its silent scream.

The Road to Takoma Park

I don't go that way
much anymore—
but I went back the other day,
to see how it had changed,
and if it still
looks the same.

There was the crossroads
where I turned,
just as drab as ever:
the same rot of parking lots,
the same strip-mall
meanness
no tangle of desert
tents or Bedouin squats
could grace—

Except a fence had been built,
to keep those
who come from places
where cars are scarce
from wandering
in the road
and being killed—

And I was on no errand
of death,
or other mission of import;

only driving home,
lost in thought—
God help me,
a dreamer . . .

What road did that last turn
take me to?
No reason for faith—
No bridge
across a gulf
that grows greater with freedom—
Only a choice,
a choice made in thin air.
Someone made that choice
for me,
someone turned my feet
for me,
and I didn't even know . . .

So I went back the other day,
to see what a shabby
stretch of road
looks like,
after a great light is gone.
It is almost the charm
of some places,
that nothing much changes them.

No vision appeared,
nor did I hear words . . .
The rest I took with me:
relief that lifted me bodily—
and an experience of
something
so good—
I wanted to lay down my soul for it.

I will come here again,
once more before I die.

Where I Live Now
Columbia Heights - Mount Pleasant, Washington DC

There was always a view from here—
Powhatan could look south
across the river, over
a far realm of blue hills
and somnolent mountains,

content with his cornfields
and palisades—
until the white men came,
with their stink and their sickly hue,
and the fever in their eyes
for whom no salted fish

to last a winter would do . . .
They built their churches
on this hill, overlooking
the moccasins and miasmas below—
and planted a grove
to memorialize the forests
that covered the continent,

they had to cut down
to fatten their coffers . . . .
The Indians are still here too,
to memorialize the shadows
that disappeared with the forest,
though they have to cross
deserts to arrive.

Some people would drive
the Indians out again,
and rid the world
of its game—
I say with an old man
who comes here today,
looking at the sky-hooks
hanging over the city:

forbear, dear friends—
let the Indian return;
it is the Great Father himself
who brings them again,
the Great Father himself
who brings nations to these shores;
let Him not wonder
if the guardians he sent
learned nothing at all—

He is the one
who sets a table in the wilderness,
bids all come, be fed.

Relation to Night

*"The self is a relation that relates itself to
its self . . . . "*

"Man is a disunity."

S. Kierkegaard, *Sickness unto Death*

I too have awakened
in the hour before light,
and lay alone with my thoughts;
when so much awaits
in the day ahead,
to think only of the day lost:
the one more day gone,
the one less to go—

Yet each day I lose
is a day gained for *them,*
everywhere in the air,
the bodiless dead,
gunned down at work,
slain in the most innocent
of routine occupations,
snared in the shadow
that made their sun bright . . .
Dread is the name
of that shadow in me.

I had a friend once
when I was a boy

who dressed all in black.
His nightmares had told him
to stop trying to run,
to listen instead
and his monsters would teach him
to *be* what he feared ...
Would that I could be that boy again,
dress all in black,
go out only at night,
be the shadow itself—
rather than the shadowed . . .

Then perhaps I would understand
why I live—
Then lifeless answers
would leap into questions,
and I would know
what questions to ask,
how to query the world,
conjure earth into hummingbirds . . .

Then in truth I would *be* alive—
Know why my feelings
rise like the tail of a peacock—
why my ideas unfold
like a page in Aladdin—

Then I would know
why relationships struggle,
why we quarrel,
lose faith in each other,
why we break up,
why like a bell
love rings with the living vibration.

Then even those
for whom the world is *too* real—
even they would know:
everything is stereoscopic
in the dislocated soul . . .

People Kaleidoscope
Boardwalk, Ocean City, Maryland, 2015

For a while it's a game:
steering through the crowd,
ears full of the thumping
of heels, gull-violins
and the tinkle and honking
of trams
that always glide up behind you
without being heard—

till I'm upside-down in my head
and I have to sit down—
enough motion around me
to enjoy without moving,
for I have been sucked
in a whirlpool of faces,
and my brain is confused . . . .

When I picture God
I see a pin-burst of colors,
too beautiful to look at—
till I steal a mirror from an apostle
and observe it reversed.
God didn't make people,
He made *Person*—
And left it to the world
to spin out the rest . . .

So why can't I see through
this sieve of savannahs
and trees?
Why do I judge people
based on their looks,
as if you were your body,
and your body, you?
I too am a body but it is
your body
that seems to confuse me.

The crowd on the boardwalk
is a clock-work of colors,
eternally unfolding—
I could watch it forever . . .
but I must get up
and move on again,
let the carousel ride
of appearances end.
As for love, what is love
but a confluence
of streams, each bearing
a leaf or a twig . . .

Will anyone bless these
streams—
or even remember the trees?

No Direction Home

"How does it feel
to be on your own,
no direction home . . . "

Bob Dylan, *Like a Rolling Stone*

I put another calendar in the drawer . . .
For a moment, a glimpse:
fifty years' worth of old
calendars, then the drawer closes.

The wind rattles its dry pods,
and I track the course
of the sun across the sky
beyond its parka of cloud.

Where I would go if I didn't come here?
The hipsters are camping
in the coffee-houses.
I pass them on the corner,
waiting for the shuttle
as I walk by to work;
they step aside as I pass,
though I am the one
who should finally step aside;
they are the ones who hurry,
clutching their coffees,
hoodies covering indifferent scrubs,
folding in the wind—

But their souls are not cold.
They have mates to find,
careers to build.
I wish them luck:
the future sits like a sphinx
on their path.
I too still have a complexity
of answers to sort.

Late roses hang over fences,
adorn small yards
like frosting on a cake;
the coals that still burn within each
warm me as I pass.
Is it enough—
to continue to exist?
A tabby observes me
from a bird-bath,
ready to jump if I pause . . .

In the small life of work,
where people who leave
die to their friends,
and some people grow old
as if old in real life,

people retreat into quiet shells
that are like glass,
decorate their offices

with crayons of children
and primitive fingerlings
of painted clay,
like grave-goods,

and become suddenly
one of those office *sadhus*
for whom any work
is no more than a day-job,

because sometimes when boundaries
blur and distinctions
fade on winter afternoons
that get in your bones,
a creature in real color
appears in a black-and-white habitat,
as if for the first time
aware of existence . . .

A man stops at a curb,
followed by ghosts in a picture frame,
forgets the light has changed . . .
Where are *my* people who hurry,
who have followed
their different ways,
like twigs on a thorn-bush?
I see their faces
in different ages of life;

they too are like ghosts now,
leaving their lives like
amputated limbs
that still twitch from time to time . . .
They are like planets now,
that follow other orbits,

leaving me to deal
with the geometry of distance.
The man at the curb
sends his glance down a street
long as a thousand blocks,
as though looking back
to the beginning of time,
and feels he is falling
in every direction at once . . .

I believe he understands:
walking the streets
is something you can only
do alone;
sometimes you are still
walking the streets, even at a desk—

But no one is really alone.
We always have our dead,
even if the only difference
is the time it takes

to reach them again,
close as the next thought,
others at the end of a text,
a call on the phone . . .

These dead of every stage
have left their warmth on my heart
that nothing will remove,
though I walk
in a thousand winter rains
with a broken umbrella . . .

This is where I live now,
as one lives at the edge
of a sea cliff,
and waits for the fog to lift—
Around me, stones
only loosely connected
slip into an abyss,
and I think for the first time,

I know this place,
I started from here . . .
I am new again, new in awareness . . .

Nabukodonozzor yanks at his leash—
lapping from a water-bowl
left in the rain.
Here is purpose at least, left to me,

We stand in front of the liquor store,
have a cloak of the light
from within,
watch the raindrops go pink
in the light of the sign,
share the joy of the bottles
on the shelves
and the lonely guests
shuttling out with their purchases—

I see a world made of glass—
I see beads on trees,
I see splintered glances
and blown-glass smiles.
The streets are glass bridges
and curbs are bevels
and the cosmos, a chandelier—
I see glass rain channeling
in fragile gutters.

I am not at home here.
I am paraplegic
in a china shop—
I am afraid to move.

Nabukodonozzor yanks me again—
And I remember,
I caught him once,
gnawing his leash.

Christmas, Rain
2015

The raindrops are bright
along the boughs of the dogwood,
but you have to watch
puddles blink
to know it is raining:
everything above ground
is the same color.

All the stores are closed
and no one's about—
except an old man
shuffling over leaf-soak,
carrying a bag
from the Million Man March . . .

But you don't know how sad
it really is
till you go to a Chinese carry-out
and they hand you
your food
from behind bullet-proof glass.

I get it this is the day
we bring presents to children—
but there is a failure
of the world

to conform to a postcard.
Even the weather
is no good
at pretending to be joyous.

An empty bus plows up the street,
shedding taillight.
For some, Christmas
merely comes
at the wrong time of day;
others wake up
to volcanic gloom.

On Coming upon a Palanquin
Columbia Road, Washington DC, October, 2012

I am writing this letter
to tell you the reason
I was late,
running to meet you—

You see, I came upon
a woman,
Our Lady of the Conquistadores,
borne down the street

by sixteen Incas
in purple and gold,
followed by a band
playing something very sad,

under sombreros,
and gray clouds
hanging low,
and drops began falling,
almost like tears,

and I stopped to watch,
—too long, perhaps—
thinking how little we know
each other's intentions,

and if you will give me
another chance
to meet you again—
if you still want my heart.

The Best Time to See Faces

Dancing down the sidewalk,
each unconscious sufferer
wanders aimlessly . . .

George Harrison,
Beware of Darkness

The best time to see faces
is a morning in winter,
when faces appear
at the top of an escalator,
rising from the ground—

You catch them as they
step off the moving plate,
jolted back to life;
the world stops moving
and they move again
under their own power—
another in the myriad
of spiritual awakenings

they will experience that day . . . .
The face I am looking for
will be consciously aware
of paper-sellers in wheelchairs,
and the morning air,
fresh as a dislocated shoulder,
but these faces hide their facts,
shutting the endlessness

of azure that is each of us
behind the mask of a job
that gives no satisfaction,
the fatigue of a night
that ended without rest . . .

I see the face of a man
who is walking with ski-poles,
his mind shows me nothing
but the uncertainty of pavement,
his eyes see the ground,
full of pigeons and wrappers,
pull his feet into eddies . . .

He will finish that nap
he started this morning,
try to get a little work done,
give thanks for the next
work-from-home day.
His wife sets a crystal,
scours the internet
for the next miracle food,

feels life growing small
within the orbit of her arms.
The wind moves a Big Gulp
closer to a scratch-off,
twists the street into space;

he knows galaxies
are coldly beautiful,
and there is no love
among the ecliptics of stars.

I see eyes that are making
a pressure-face:
they belong to a woman
holding something inside,
for the ride has been long.
This is the kind of pain
it is useful to focus on,
the kind of pain you
can do something about;
it gives you the look
of having a purpose in life,

—or perhaps it's only cancer,
a hermit-crab in her heart
trying to pinch its way out,
like a bladder
you don't want to empty,
something you need
to hold in, a last breath,
the last spark of a thought
you don't want to release,
hurrying to find a place
that doesn't exist for the living—

till whatever it was
is released like a dam,
and disappears in the ground . . .

A woman with a stroller,
a teddy-bear in the stroller
and a child at her side:
her face is alive.
Her eyes are like lions
that look out over a plain,
gathering the reins
of its life in their gaze—

but these eyes are not looking for food.
Look, Honey, show Teddy
the corner where the homeless
man lives,
he is a hoarder,
the whole world is his hoard-space;

look, Honey, show Teddy
the man who is cursing
a friend on his cell,
no one understands
how hard it is to be poor,
anger is the only thing
they have enough of;

look, Honey, show Teddy
the man in the fez
on a motorized recliner,
see him go flying
scattering the pigeons
on his throne of the flesh;

—but Teddy doesn't care.
His button-down eyes
seem to stare
or gently cross
at an emptiness beyond them . . .

Young faces appear,
the same somber expressions.
Four of the seven doors
of their souls are closed:
ears by ear-buds,
eyes by their devices.
They are like people already
old, coming to work

without their spectacles on . . . .
The water-bottles or coffee
they clutch are the river
that floats them along.

The low sun throws
shadows on a steam-grate;
their ambition in life
is to make the mist visible
as they vanish,
as if through sheers . . .

The flower-seller sitting
beside a wagon-load of roses
shows a mouth without teeth.
He has a shunt in his arm,
no valid beliefs.
But I am tired

of looking at faces—
I can only love them
by watching them,
and they wouldn't understand.
I am like a pigeon
with a foot in a grate,
struggling to escape.
My soul has its wings,
but no air to fly.

Kite Sky

6th Street & Boardwalk,
Ocean City, Maryland, 2015

"Sky of my delight . . . "
Jenni Moore Crocker

The sky was crowded—
it looked like a Times Square
of kites in the air . . .
But you couldn't look up;
you'd be knocked down

by the crowd on the shore,
shuffling along,
sunburned and bored,
wondering how joy
had eluded them again . . .

Still I saw what the wind
that blows here from Florida
conceals in its robes,
when it slips out of clothes
and goes naked as a god . . .

Would that I could be here
a morning in May,
when the wind is still
cold, and no summer sounds
tamp down the surf,

to watch how like sailors
they get those things up—
Perhaps then I would think
of the winds in our lives,

if we could see the colorful
parasails they hide—
or get a desire
like one of these seamen,
to unfurl a spinner
on a blustery day,
and celebrate the sky . . .

Under Lake Water

Lago di Brocciano, Italy, 1953

Under lake water
I found a ring,
gold and bright,
a fortune to a child.

Under that water
German barges slept,
full of munitions
for boys to find,
guarded by sunfish.

But I thought of how
a gelato would taste,
so I gave it to Dad.
Pawn it for me, I said.
He gave me a buck.

Mom gave me a ring too.
Go to a pawn shop,
see what you can get—
It had been a long time
since I thought of that lake,
diving for bullets,

but still I remembered
those bubble-seeded
grenades,

mossy shells still
able to explode,
habitat for minnows.

Eulogy for a Businessman
who Jumped off a Bridge

Permit me, Augusto,
to inhabit your life,
since you are no longer using it—
I will make up your life,
in my playing-acting fashion,

and get it all wrong—but
Augusto, though we never met,
let me be your medium:
use the voice of one
who was blind to you in life,

you who are now body-blind—
If your restless soul passes
this way, use me, Augusto,
to leave behind the message
you didn't leave in life,

or at least one clue
to the six-figure world;
let me mime your life
that was lived in deadly earnest—
tell me a secret so those
who are suffering will know
this is not imagination,
like one who steals something
left lying on the ground . . .

Tell me how, in that last dream,
in that last night of your life
that seemed to go on so long,
and that only got darker
before the sun finally rose,
you saw the listings
on the board of an exchange,

and they were all names,
some men you knew, many
you didn't, and your own name,
there, among all the others,
and the names all had numbers . . .

Tell me too of that ladder
to the clouds, and of the
shadowy figures going up
and coming down—
and how firm the ladder is,

the hand of God holding it;
anyone can be forgiven
for having this dream, and certainly,
Augusto, you were not the first
to feel the firmness of God,
too firm for most lives . . .

And tell me at last, Augusto,
  of the existence of gravity,

and what a blessing it is
we don't go floating into space;
how God gave us order,
and when we have wings
we can fly,
and when we don't, it will kill us . . .

Why Confederate Memorials Should Remain on a Battlefield

Gettysburg, Pennsylvania, July 3rd, 2015

It didn't look like this,
during the battle—
the guide pointed out across the field:
showing farmland
that didn't look different
from any other farmland . . .

coarse grain waist-high,
trees crouching
in black-green masses,
the usual fences and barns,
just their tops peeking up;
it was hotter than a hayrick
on fire that summer,
and little Round Top
was covered with rocks.

All that would change of course.
First to go,
the hypnosis of cicadas,
climbing out of the ground
to the tops of trees,
and returning to the ground again,
the sound of the land itself,

till cannon shook them out—
after that, the silence . . .

the silence of a century of noonings.
They came up to a white land
to find dark sleep,
roads just about ready
for their first horseless carriages.

The battle itself
was a disjointed affair,
one minute jogging,
then the order to fall out,
echoes flying over
like rounds of artillery,
then double-time again—
Limbs were being cut off
with wires;
the men who were bleeding out
called for water.

The next day was rain;
hate would be awakened
by no one who fought here.
The North needed
to honor their courage—
It was no accident
a beast walked the land,
leaving the fields
littered with cenotaphs . . . .

Molly in the Alps
Sustenpass, Switzerland 2015

"Be strong and courageous. Do not be
afraid or terrified, for the Lord your
God is with you wherever you go; He
will never leave you nor forsake you –"

Deuteronomy 31:6.

Girl, what do these megaliths
have to do with you,
rising like titans'-teeth
to swallow the sky?

God made these hills,
that to us are stupendous,
when he stirred in his sleep
and one eyelid
brushed the earth.

Girl, you found a new way
to pray, told not to pray
in the angles of streets,
as the hypocrites pray.

You go in front of mountains
and pray,
dead in your tracks,
arms hung in awe.

Girl, you may indeed
be seen of men,
but all this is inside your heart,
these rocks, this ice,
these giants of the sky—

Their bellowed praise
is only heard
in hearts of faith:
Fear not—
God will keep you safe.

Tiger Balm Gardens

"Scenes of Chinese mythology, folklore,
legends & Confucian philosophy."

Singapore, 1956

1

Come take a ride
in a Chinese amusement park—

Take a ride on the coolie slalom,
their hats thrown back,
their pig-tails a-flying,
all the coolies a-running—

the whole family running:
mama coolie running,
sister coolie running,
brother coolie running,

only papa not running;
papa on his back,
one foot in the air,
his little toe off—

2

Take a ride in the tunnel of love,
a moonlit night at sea,
no storm in sight—
nothing to disturb
the silvery waves,
thousands of geishas
a-swim in the moon-path,

even the ship on its side
seems to restfully sink,
a ferry going down,
feeding its passengers
to the arms of the geishas . . .

and the teeth of the sharks,
restfully floating
in the troughs of the sea,
foamy with red-froth,

3

Take a ride on the Mama-San cars,
putting down her towel
to come a-running from the door—
Li Mei's little head
left behind by a bus,

and the frozen crowd—
the innocent bus
at the end of the block—
and Li Mei's little brains,
running like egg-yolk . . .

4

Take a walk on the midway,
when a tropical torrent
bends down the fronds,
then dry in an instant—
All the painted pagodas
explode in a jungle,
they call it Happy-Luck . . .

Night at the Symphony

Schumann's No. 3, known as the "Renish"

If I were asleep,
I would be having a tone-dream,
ten-thousand voices
speaking at once,
but I am at the symphony,
my thoughts
floating away from me . . .

The seats are still filling.
People are coming in
as if out of a downpour,
though this rain is dry:
nothing grows
in this rain
except concrete and stone.

If *my* life were music,
a ballerina would dance
on sparklets of glass,
the Great Bear
her tiara
and a glitter of frost, her gown,
and the homeless would watch.

What does it mean,
this swelling and falling,
conjured by music-sticks

like kelp on a sea floor?
The tone-charms subside
but no vision appears.

I know music is more
than just playing a long time,
but my ears are blind.
I look at the faces
of the people around me,
ponder what images
grow from closed eyes.

Astrological

for Theodoric

You who were born
in the sign of the goat-fish,
you are a hybrid.
Heights are not new to you—
To get to the bottom,
you merely stand on your head.

You were the one
who went in with Granddad,
disappearing in the hole
of the Sinks of Gandy,
while the green hills
dotted with cattle and daubs
of trees, and a blue height
docked with clouds,

restrained your brother and me.
Granddad came back for you
while you were asleep,
and I am pulled backward,
into your shadow.

From the lowest of hollows
and under low boughs
and the bottoms of bushes,
last sparks rise like
left-behind souls,

while the tops of the trees
call them to hasten.

The last message you sent
said "Tomorrow"—
Tomorrow you will tell me
where you have been.
Tomorrow we will meet again
on a green lawn
Tomorrow you will come back to me.

Corn Plant

The corn plant I gave you
twenty years ago—
have you seen it today,
taller than I am now,
between the window and the bed?

Did you see it has a flower,
after all these years?
I potted it for you,
and we moved in together.
Now the children are gone.
Still it grows on alone.

Such a fever-sweet scent,
the smell of tropical rain,
those balls of tiny stars,
big dandelion puffs—
it catches you up
when you walk through the door,

it perfumes the room,
and I smell it in my sleep.
I awake in the dark
when there are no more dreams
to remember,
only the long years past,

themselves now a dream,
What does it mean,
blooming now,
all those years with no bloom?

To the runner goes the laurel,
to the dancer, bouquets.
I think I know now
why they bring flowers to the dead . . .

Watching Snow Fall at Work

It is snowing outside.
The weather is having
an old-fashioned pillow fight.
Snow is cooling on ledges
in old-fashioned loaves.

The snowflakes are waving
a mesmerist's chain—
Some flakes grow confused,
lose their direction,
try to go back . . .
Others grow heavy
in personal downwardness.
The world in its white
is as elegant as a wedding gown.

But somewhere across Siberia
lights are on early:
the shuffle of stockinged feet,
already begun,
the sound of ghosts . . .
confronting the befuddlement
of a locked door,
coming back to haunt them.

Here the living return
to their desks,
thinking anew

of how far they live,
how fast snow falls—
An unequal race
only those who never leave
can win . . .

The Cave at Grotto Bay

Long Island, Bahamas

They name everything on this island:
a cat called Driftwood,
A turtle named Bombardier,
Charlemagne the rooster,
Vodun the goat,
—except for the bats,
too numerous to name,
and the snake in the cave.

They say you'll see the snake
in the beam of your light,
its multifarious folds
sliding away
in different directions,
to go deeper in the dark.
I haven't seen it myself—
I don't care to go in,
and it has no need to come out.

The day ends in dusky quiet,
the bats on their springs,
happy to be alive,
and I hear a last sigh
as of the sea settling down,
and feel a last breeze . . . .

It is then that I think
the whole world is a cave,
and we are like bats,
returning to sleep
in the safety of vaults
and other high thoughts—

Till we grow old,
and the darkness gathers beneath us . . .

Samhain
October 31, 2014

There were no bonfires on Hobart Street . . .
but there could have been:
people were out as if in a forest,

and the street was blocked off
with a yellow tape—
and a thousand carved embers
burned

up and down in the dark,
as if a climate suddenly favorable
for children
had been created,
out of the ashes of something . . .

Old things always
get passed down to children.
This night was no different.
Even the adults
were dressed up like children

in wizard hats
and krazy-kat stovepipes,
guiding their steps
up and down the block,
picking their houses,

rehearsing the charm
they will utter at each door . . .

For this night is Samhain,
first night of nights—
The first night you leave work
and it's already dark,
the first night you feel cold,
the first night something
happens,
before you feel ready . . .

Poetry is Mindfulness

*Ma Virgilio n'avea lasciati scemi
di sé . . .*

Purgatorio, Canto XXX

Come—
I've been your guide
through the worst of it;
this won't be as bad.
We'll have to do a little
climbing, of course;
we'll take it easy at first.
Hold my hand if you wish . . .

Another load of immigrants
arrives, fading as they pass,
like smoke-breath
in the hint
of a January dawn.
They never lived anyway,
the moment it was happening . . .

No carry-ons please,
backpacks, trolley-totes,
suitcases on wheels—
Throw out the past,
forget the future.
If you bring anything,
bring only the now.

Dear God, can that really
be me—? Crushed
under the weight of my cares,
or my eyes sewn shut
by a rose or a sunrise,
or running the marathon
of endless successes,
or walking in the flame
of perpetual desire—?

An Indian war bonnet
hangs on the feeder,
full of life;
flits off in its own breeze
and cracks a seed,
a sheaf of blue feathers,
aimed at the sky—

Now that you've seen him,
your hand holds only air,
for I will be gone.
This threshold beads
with your presence.
All you see now is your own.

Season of Lights
December, 2014

Salt stained streets,
pot-holes, scraps of sooty snow
in parking-lots—

Let summer's blaze
depart.
The source of all light
pays a visit to the earth

when nights are dark,
in glowing sleet,
gingerbread mansions,
clown-tears
on a dying bush . . .

and calls us to report.

Dean's Blue Hole
Long Island, Bahamas

To Donita Faye, Dierdre Vashti,
Renee Monique, Nick Mevoli and
Theron Maillis

There is no shade on this beach.
The bright sun beats
the low scrub to the sand.
If you want shade,
you have to go into the hole.

Donita, Dierdre, Renee,
did you too feel
the call of that shade?
One by one you
stepped into the water,
holding hands to the end.
Now the hole calls you its own.

Nick Mevoli, the world
watched you die.
You only wanted one thing,
and what you wanted, it gave.
When you came up,
it had doubled itself
in your eyes,
but those holes weren't for seeing . . .

Theron Maillis, you who were the youngest—
you were an island boy.
What was it you forgot,
that last time you came up?
Did you leave a part of yourself
behind?
They say you were in a hurry
to go back,
and never returned.

Canal Walk
C & O Canal, February 2004

What a crowd there was
along the towpath—
leafless trees above,
the river broad
between gray banks,
parade of bicycle and dog.

Who told the world to
come to this place,
disturbing winter sleep
of crow and sycamore,
and the slow decay
of an engineering marvel,
our pyramid and coliseum,
rolled into one?

Once this land
was an ocean of trees,
settlers pale and sickly
in its gloom
of green summers,
Indians hiking its ridges,
traders leading pack-mules
into solitary years . . .

Now the balance is tipped—
Nothing but people,

the land disappeared.
Drab skies breed boredom
with an empty ditch.
We are our own wilderness.

Cat Sanctuary
Largo di Torre Argentina, Rome, October, 2014

It's been sixty years
since I was last in this city,
so first thing I did
when I got off the plane,
I went to Largo Argentina
to visit the cats.

It's a window into the past,
this city block exposed
to the ground below—
if the past was jumbled
ruins,

broken columns of goddesses,
stone blocks
warming in the sun,
blue sky and umbrella-pines
over the hall
where Caesar died,

and cats—
ancient citizens of history,
wise as lares,
numerous as monkeys
in a Hindu temple.

They were here when Cato
dived on his sword,
and Cicero kindly
lent his head to the Forum,

and an American boy,
who knew nothing
of history,
came with sardines
to sleepy sun-worshippers,

and almost lost a finger,
trying to feed them—

Beach Walk, Night
with BHC again

The wind picks up
as the light fades,
blows you
against my shoulder;
the day's warmth
retreats
to the nook between our palms,
the only place
it can still live in the cold,

and like the waves
that hide
what's left of the light
in playful foam,
joins us in a
phosphorescent glow
we lose too soon—

Your lips on mine
would save this
moment out of time,
like our mingled
footprints in the sand,
swept away too soon—

But look—
the stars like sand so thick!

The whole night sky's
a shore,
and there they stay.

Salon

U St NW, Washington DC

It is morning and
a mirror is before me.
Is today the day
the mirror will give me
its answer:
how long I can go
before getting my hair cut?

I know a place
where the young are like
the gods
of the summer storm,
blowing through the hair-dryers
and water,
and the sun breaking through
in all the mirrors,
after the downpour.

In front of *this* mirror
someone has just
opened a grave—
Meanwhile the style-girls
are manifold in *their* beams,
and I am surrounded
by opposites
in every surface.

I watched the style-girl
chewing her gum;
you can never
tell what they're thinking,
shampooing your hair,
silently cutting,
considering their judgments—

But the style-boys,
dishing with their clients—
How safe they must feel,
to love the sameness in another.
But do they too tire
of that fountain
that wears down its basin
and every stone
bowl
that tries to contain it,
with its pitiless jets—?

I leave there
like a shorn ram
out of a flaming chute,
glad to be free
for another six months—
And breathed a prayer
to my patron

saint of hair-cutting,
St Anthony of the Desert Fathers,

how they beset
him, who were after all
only his own desires
manifest—
How they beat him,
and rudely tugged
his beard,
and maybe even tried
to give him a trim . . .

Theater Without Seats

House Concert, April, 2016

The thing about theater
everyone thinks
is that everything's scripted,
but that's not the thing—
The thing is something
else.

A woman sat in a silent
room, everyone waiting . . .
Then she began
and guitar notes sprayed
like sound-drops,
surprising our ears.
Her voice submerged us too
in a sustained high tone

and seductive bases,
telling us her tales
that had to be sung to be heard.
And we sat, silent,
while ghostly figures strayed
before us,
imprisoned in our hearing.

Like these roaming forms
of sound that live
only in our ears,
we too have been sung

into existence,
live only in the one ear
that hears our speech.

How do friendships change
that are not free
to grow, or confined?
Surely for that night
one singer
voiced her spell,
and our affections knew.

But did they too, those
fleeting sound-forms,
feel they were under
the lights of a stage,
no audience, no playbook,
no plot,
just a frame of stage-flats
and a made space,

where instead of flowing away,
awareness folds back
on its own scene,
giving stutter to words,
shade to gestures,
hesitation to glances
that should have been clear—?

Tell your singer to sing me
a new song,
a song about love:
two bodies unable
to occupy the same space,
and two souls who do—

And I will forget
that old song,
that song about the road,
you know the one—
"Lord I'm five
hundred miles from my home . . . "

Book of a Dream

I had a dream and
in my dream I was sitting
around with some friends
and in a bit out of
Alice I'd stolen some
body's bon-bons and
my irises were making
like pinwheels
in a high wind but
I couldn't admit it—
I didn't want people
to know I was a thief,

but everyone else
had eaten the bon-bons
too and were afraid
to be found out,
so we all had to pretend
nothing was wrong
and it wasn't much fun
to tell you the truth,
in fact it was a drag—

Then I dreamed I
woke up and
went out for a walk
to chase the dream
from my head—

but everyone who comes
into the world
is in a place where
he doesn't belong,
so what good was that?
No one wants

to be the first to
tell the world that
existence is a fish-bowl,
and like Dylan says
we're all doing
our best to deny it—
and besides being
a total waste of bon-bons,
the dream always
ends badly because
when you wake up you
die.

Eulogy for Margaret Hunter Pierce

In death even
as in life
she confounded her detractors,

remaining unclaimed
because no
one could agree what had killed her,

till, in the end,
they settled on one
word: *old,*
and let it go at that.

What one knew
about her one
knew only from
rumors
and what happened in print;

what *she* knew
about herself she
knew only from
rumors
and what happened in print:

how
she been born
too soon,

how they had
fed her with an eye-dropper,
how her father had
said
she would never be
right, how
her mother didn't

want her,
how she had confounded
them all—

until even she had exhausted
every possibility,
and all that was left
were the rumors
and what happened in print.

It took a hundred
speeches
and a whole
day
to consign them to oblivion;

it took one
minute

in the middle of the night
to write down this,

an epitaph—
And I thank her for that.